BUDDHIST TEXTS QUOTED AS SCRIPTURE

BUDDHIST TEXTS QUOTED AS SCRIPTURE

BY THE

GOSPEL OF JOHN:

A DISCOVERY IN THE LOWER CRITICISM

ALBERT J EDMUNDS

GYAN

Published by

Gyan Publishing House
5, Ansari Road
Daryaganj, New Delhi-110002
Phone: 011-47034999, 9811692060
E-mail: books@gyanbooks.com

Distribution Network
gyanbooks.com
India, USA, Canada, UK, Australia

ISBN: 978-93-6433-160-9 (HB)

First Published, 1906

2nd Impression 2025

Printed at: Gyan Press, Delhi.

BUDDHIST TEXTS QUOTED AS SCRIPTURE
Author: ALBERT J EDMUNDS

Buddhist Texts Quoted as Scripture

BY THE

GOSPEL OF JOHN:

a discovery in the lower criticism.

(*John VII. 38; XII. 34.*)

By ALBERT J. EDMUNDS,

Author of Buddhist and Christian Gospels.

PHILADELPHIA:

MAURICE BRIX, 129 South Fifteenth Street, and A. J. EDMUNDS,

241 West Duval Street.

1906.

Dedicated to my friend MAURICE BRIX.

PREFACE.

Since the manuscript of *Buddhist and Christian Gospels* was despatched to Japan in September, 1904, I have continued to find parallels between the two great religions. A remarkable one, discovered this spring in a Buddhist book newly published by the London Pāli Text Society, has called forth the present essay. For fuller information my readers must refer to the Tōkyō book.

Our somewhat provincial education has not yet made us realize that, at the time of Christ, India was one of the four great Powers of the earth. The other three were China, Rome and Parthia. But India was the greatest intellectually, and her then most popular religion, Buddhism, was the dominant spiritual force upon the continent of Asia.

It is to be regretted that so few theologians and even Orientalists are acquainted with Pāli literature Our culture has too long been bounded by the River Euphrates, and the central fact of the world's religious history has not yet taken its place in the historical imagination of Europe and America. That central fact is this :—The two greatest missionary religions, each emanating from a wonderful personality, started from the Holy Land of antiquity,* and proceeded in opposite directions around the

---

*The region between the Ganges and the Nile. See Buddhist and Christian Gospels, Historical Introduction.

world. Each went as far as it could go until it reached the Pacific Ocean; and now, in Japan and the United States, these two great world-faiths are facing each other. Henceforth the Pacific Ocean, instead of the Mediterranean Sea, must be the centre of our culture; and the two religions, instead of being enemies, must be friends.

241 West Duval Street,
Germantown:
May 30—July 4, 1906.

BUDDHIST TEXTS QUOTED AS SCRIPTURE

BY THE GOSPEL OF JOHN.

It is well known, that there are, in the New Testament, quotations from other literatures than the Hebrew and the books of its Canon, as when Paul quotes the Greek poet Aratus (1) and Jude the apocryphal book of Enoch. (2)

In the Gospel of Mark there is a quotation, as if from Scripture, which does not occur in the Old Testament, but which Rendel Harris discovered in a midrash on Genesis ascribed to Philo. (3) It evidently emanates from some early commentary or apocryphal work known to the Evangelist.

MARK IX. 13.

I say unto you, that Elijah is come, and they have also done unto him whatsoever they listed, *even as it is written of him.*

Nowhere does the Old Testament foretell that the second Elijah will be persecuted. The quotation is therefore apocryphal or extra-Judaic.

---

(1) Acts XVII. 28.

(2) Jude 14 and 15.

(3) Philonis Judæi Alexandrini libri Antiquitatum, Quæstionum et Solutionum in Genesin. Basileæ, 1527, folio.

Scholars have long been accustomed to such quotations, and are not astonished thereat when they spring from the literature that surrounded the Judæans. But modern research has made it clear that a wider range of influence affected the composition of the New Testament than the books of the Hebrews, the Greeks and the Romans. Heretofore, these have been our three classic nations, and their common lake, the Mediterranean, has been our central sea; but since the acquisition of India by the English in 1757, and especially since that of the Philippines by ourselves, the sacred books of Asia have widened our horizon. The Pacific Ocean is now our central sea, and to our classical peoples we have added several more, with India first and foremost. We have found that India was the home of the ancient fable, the mother of Æsop and of the Arabian Nights. A folk-lorist has traced Indian fables in the Jewish Talmud, one of which can be dated at A. D. 118. (4)

Three stories in the Christian Apocryphal Gospels are also found in that great Buddhist apocryphal gospel, the *Lalita Vistara*, (5) which contains a

---

(4) See Æsop's Fables. Edited by Joseph Jacobs. London, 1889.

(5) These stories are: the obeisance of idols to the Divine Child in a temple; his supernatural knowledge of the alphabet; and his being lost by his parents and found engaged in religious activity. These parallels will all be fully treated in my next edition of Buddhist and Christian Gospels. My attention has been directed to them by the works of Pfleiderer and Van Eysinga.

poetical account of Buddha's early life, and was translated into Chinese in the seventh century, while a legendary life of Buddha, closely akin, was translated in the sixties of the first century.

It has also been discovered that the life of Buddha was translated into the language of Persia quite early in our era, and worked up into a Christian romance called *Barlaam and Joasaph.* This ancient church novel was popular all over Europe throughout the middle ages, from Greece to Iceland, while so late as the eighteenth century a Jesuit bearing the historic name of Borgia translated it into the Tagalog of the Philippine Islands! The name Joasaph or Josaphat (for it is written both ways) has been proven to be a corruption of the Sanskrit Bodhisattva, a title of the youthful Buddha; and the Indian saint, under this disguise, was canonized by both Greek and Roman Churches. On the twenty-sixth of August in the Eastern communion and on the twenty-seventh of November in the Western, we have the singular spectacle of Catholic priests commemorating the Hindu thinker as a Christian saint.

Now it has been cogently argued by a European scholar (6) that if Christendom could thus borrow from Buddhism in the sixth century, it could do the same in the first, for the same channels of intercourse were open. Indeed at the time of Christ this intercourse was at its height, for the geographer

---

(6) Van Eysinga, in his work on Hindu Influence upon the Gospels. 1901 and 1904.

Strabo, who was writing in the twenties of the first century, when the youthful Jesus was a carpenter in Galilee, saw one hundred and twenty ships prepared to sail from a Red Sea port to India.

If this be the case, we need not be astonished at the following Buddhist text embedded in the Gospel of John, that most mystic and recondite of the four, charged, as it is, with the philosophy of Ephesus and Alexandria, where the thought of all nations found a home.

MIRACULOUS WATER PROCEEDS FROM THE SAINT.

John VII. 38. He that believeth on me, as the Scripture hath said, out of his belly shall flow rivers of living water.

THE WAY TO SUPERNAL KNOWLEDGE

(*Paṭisambhidā-maggo*) *I. 53.*

What is the Tathāgato's knowledge of the twin miracle? In this case, the Tathāgato works a twin miracle unrivalled by disciples: from his upper body proceeds a flame of fire, *and from his lower body proceeds a torrent of water.* Again, from his lower body proceeds a flame of fire, and from his upper body a torrent of water.

Here the words of John, *ποταμοι 'εκ της κοιλιας αυτου ρευσουσιν ὑδατος* equate the Pāli *hetthimakâyato udaka-*

dhârâ pavattati, except for the tense and number, and the word "proceed" or "roll forth," instead of "flow," and "lower body" instead of "belly." (7) The addition of ζωντος in the Greek is the only word which can be ascribed to the Old Testament: "living water" occurs in several of the prophets. But the quotation as a whole is not there. Dean Alford, in his commentary, voices the despair of all the exegetes from the beginning, when he says: "We look in vain for such a text in the Old Testament, and an apocryphal or lost canonical book is out of the question." The learned dean interprets by making the body refer to the under part of the temple in an oracle of Ezekiel, wherein that mystic beholds rivers of living water preceeding from beneath the holy place. But no such far-fetched theory is needful any longer, now that we have found a Buddhist oracle almost verbally coincident.

In a book of Buddhist legends called *Avadânas* is one entitled *sûtra* instead of *avadâna*, thus aiming at canonical rank. (8) This is the *Prâtihârya Sûtra*, i. e. SACRED BOOK ABOUT MIRACLES. It is also embedded in the canonical Book of Discipline of a sect whose recension of the scriptures of Buddhism has been lost in the original Pāli or Sanskrit, but preserved in Chinese and Tibetan. This Book of Miracles relates that Buddha sent forth fire and water from his person, and produced other startling phenomena to confound unbelievers. All sects did not admit the story into the Canon, for in the Pāli Book of Discipline, transmitted by the school of

(7) See Appendix B.
(8) " " "

the Elders, at the very point in the text where the legend occurs in the Tibetan version, there is reported a miracle by a disciple which Buddha sternly forbade. However, albeit uncanonical according to the conservative Elders, the story is ancient and appears in Açvaghosha's first-century poem, (9) while it is evidently understood in the text above quoted from the *Way to Supernal Knowledge*. Moreover, it is ranked with the Canonical life-scenes in a Ceylon temple-sculpture of the second century before Christ. According to the Great Chronicle,

" The miracle under the mango-tree " (10)

was graven upon the Great Tope at Anurādhapura, together with the incidents that follow it in the Miracle Sūtra. These sculptures are buried or destroyed, but the extant remains at Bharahat and Sāñci prove that the whole legend of Buddha's early life was already highly developed at the time of Christ. (See Appendix.)

The Fourth Evangelist transfigures the passage, and converts the miraculous torrent of the magus into a spiritual river. The single adjective "living," with its prophetic associations, is enough to exalt the whole conception into a loftier sphere. At the same time we must remember that the Buddhists also found mystical meanings in their Scriptures, and produced their Philos and their Origens, as we shall some day realize more fully, when the vast literature preserved in Chinese is made known to Europe and America. Living water or immortal drink is also a Buddhist phrase, and in the Realist

(9) See Appendix B.
(10) " " "

Book of Discipline (Tibetan) it is applied to Nirvā*n*a. The conception that lies behind the legend of the Twin Miracle is that of the microcosm: the saint is conceived as uniting in himself all nature, and hence in the water-meditation he is assimilated to water, and in the flame-meditation he passes away in fire.

Be it observed that, in the Pāli text, this miracle is "unrivalled by disciples," and indeed the summing up expressly says that Buddhas alone can perform it. But in the Book of Avadānas, which has Realist affinities, the Buddhist Daniel performs the Twin Miracle:

> From half of his body the water did rain;
> From half did the fire of a sacrifice blaze.

Moreover, in the Pāli texts themselves, Dabbo the Mallian emits fire from his fingers to light the monks to bed, and finally passes away in the flame-meditation, a veritable Buddhist Elijah.

Similarly in the Gospel, the believer can accomplish the water-miracle, though of course in a mystical sense, in accordance with the higher plane of the Fourth Evangelist. Moreover, the latter is probably quoting some Buddhist collection belonging to the Realist school, which predominated in Northwestern India, where the Greek empire adjoined. It is almost certain that such a collection had found its way westward in the *Yonaloko,* perhaps in Greek, perhaps in Syriac. The recent discovery of Manichæan Scriptures in Chinese

Turkestan has prepared us for anything in the way of ancient distribution of sacred literature.

Now, while one case of the mysterious Fourth Evangelist quoting a Buddhist text as Scripture would be remarkable, two such cases are significant, and almost certainly imply historical connection, *especially when taken together with the fact that other parts of the Gospels present verbal agreements with Pâli texts.* And there is one other case where the Gospel of John quotes a Buddhist oracle as Scripture. It was first pointed out in the Chicago *Open Court* for February, 1900. Indeed it was placed at the very outset of my first series of *Gospel Parallels from Pâli texts.* It has been reprinted in subsequent editions of that collection, and last appeared in the third edition of Buddhist and Christian Gospels (Tōkyō, 1905, p. 146.) It is here reprinted and amplified :—

THE CHRIST REMAINS [on earth] FOR THE ÆON.

John XII. 34. The multitude therefore answered him, We have heard out of the law, that the Christ abideth forever [εἰς τον αἰωνα, *for the æon.*]

Enunciations VI. I, and Long Collection, Dialogue 16 (*Book of the Great Decease.* Translated in Sacred Books of the East, Vol. XI, p. 40.)

Ānando, any one who has practised the four principles of psychical power, — developed them, made them active and practical, pursued

them, accumulated and striven to the height thereof,—can, if he so should wish, remain [on earth] for the æon or the rest of the æon.

Now, Ānando, the Tathāgato has practised and perfected these; and if he so should wish, *the Tathāgato could remain* **[on earth]** *for the æon* **or the rest of the æon.**

The words in italics agree with those in the Greek of John, except the mood and tense of the verb. Rendel Harris has pointed out to me that the tense of μενει is ambiguous, being either present or future. This is because the oldest manuscripts are without accents. Tathāgato is a religious title equivalent to Christ. Its exact meaning is still debated, but its analogy to Sugato is obvious, and Rhys Davids' translation of it as *Truth-winner* is probably as near the mark as we shall ever get.

As our text occurs also in the Sanskrit of the Book of Avadānas (which has an independent transmission) its antiquity is certain. Moreover, the Book of the Great Decease and that of Enunciations are two of the oldest in the Pāli, Enunciations being also one of the Nine Divisions of a lost arrangement of the Canon.

The ascription of the saying in John to "the multitude" shows it to have been a current belief at the time of Christ. It is not a New Testament doctrine, though the physical Second Coming has been assimilated to it. Commentators have been at a loss to identify the Old Testament passage ("out of the Law") which is supposed to be quoted. The Twentieth Century New Testament proposes the Aramaic version of Isaiah IX. 7 as the source. The learned August Wünsche, in his work on the Gospels and the Talmud, says that the source is unknown. Be that as it may, we have here a verbal Pāli parallel :—

ὁ Χριστος μενει εἰς τον αἰωνα = *Tathâgato kappa*m *ti*tt*heyya*.

A kindred sentiment appears at the conclusion of Matthew :

Lo, I am with you alway, even unto the end of the æon.

If we could be sure that the Evangelist was copying this from the lost Mark-ending or from the Logia, we could pronounce it a first-century document and an utterance of the Lord ; but we cannot, and most Matthæan additions to the Synoptical record are suspect. It is quite likely that these words were added to the First Gospel after the appearance of the Fourth, with its doctrine of the Paraclete. On the other hand, we can date the first translation of the corresponding Buddhist doctrine into Chinese at about A. D. 68, and this in a popular manual which presupposes the vast body of the Sūtras. (See note 18.)

Another verbal agreement between John and the Pāli texts (though not expressly quoted) is given in Buddhist and Christian Gospels, p. 138 :—

I have overcome the world.

In the Johannine spirit is :—

He who sees the truth sees me.

(Op. cit. p. 150.)

The following Parallels are also Johannine :—

No. 29. Disciples repelled by deep doctrine.
" 42. The Saviour is unique.
" 44. The Light of the World.
" 45. I am a King.
" 47. The Master remembers a pre-existent state.
" 48. Knowing God and his Kingdom.
" 51. The Master can Renounce or prolong his Life.
" 58. In the World, but not of the World

Another noteworthy parallel, with some verbal agreements, is found in certain phrases of Luke's angelic Birth-Hymn, as was pointed out in my pamphlet of 1905. (11)

Luke II. 8-14.

And there were shepherds in the same country abiding in the field, and keeping watch by night over their flock. And an *angel* of the Lord stood by them, and the glory of the Lord shone round about them : and they were sore afraid. And the angel said unto them, Be not afraid ; for behold, I bring you good tidings of

(11) *Can the Pâli Pitakas aid us in fixing the Text of the Gospels ?* Philadelphia, 1905, 8 vo. pp. 8.

great joy which shall be to all the people: for *there is born* to you this day *in the city of* David a Saviour, which is *Christ* the Lord. And this is the sign unto you: Ye shall find a babe wrapped in swaddling clothes, and lying in a manger. And suddenly there was with the angel a multitude of *the heavenly host praising* God, and saying,

Glory to God in the highest,
And on earth peace, divine favor among men.

Sutta Nipāto, Mahāvaggo, Nālaka-Suttam.

The heavenly hosts, rejoicing, delighted,
And Sakko the leader and *angels* white-stoled,
Seizing their robes, and *praising* exceedingly,
Did Asito the hermit see in noonday rest.

[He asks the angels why they rejoice, and they answer:]

The *Buddha-to-be*, the best and matchless Jewel,
Is born for weal and welfare in the world of men,
In the town of the Sākyas, in the region of Lumbinī:
Therefore are we joyful and *exceeding glad.*

The parallel is further carried out in the narrative: the hermit, like the shepherds, goes to pay his reverence to the newborn Saviour.

Here the Greek ἐπι της γης εἰρηνη, ἐν ἀνθρωποις εὐδοκια appears to be a reminiscence of the Pâli *manussa-loke hitasukhatâya*, "for weal and welfare in the world of men," an oft-repeated phrase in the Pâli texts.

Another verbal parallel will be found in my Japanese book, at p. 213. I here reprint it, with slight changes, from the *Open Court*, where it first appeared, in April, 1900:—

AN ÆON-LASTING SIN.

Mark III. 29. Whosoever shall blaspheme against the Holy Spirit hath never forgiveness, but is guilty of an æon-lasting sin.

Cullavaggo VII. 3. (Translated in S. B. E. XX. p. 254.)

Is it true, Devadatto, as they say, that thou goest about to stir up schism in the Order and schism in our society?—It is true, Lord.—Enough, Devadatto. Let not schism in the Order be pleasing unto thee: serious, O Devadatto, is a schism in the Order. Whosoever, Devadatto, divides the Order when it is at peace gives birth to *an æon-lasting fault*, and for an æon he is tormented in hell. But whosoever, Devadatto, makes peace in the Order when it has been divided gives birth to the highest merit (literally, Brahmâ-merit), and for an æon he is happy in paradise.

The words αἰωνιον ἁμαρτημα in Mark III. 29, are the exact verbal equivalent of the Pâli *kappa*tt*hika*m *kibbisa*m, or, as the Siam edition has it, *kappa*tt-*hitika*m. Schism is the deadly sin of Buddhism, the other four of its deadly sins being rare deeds of violence—matricide, parricide, saint-murder and wounding a Buddha. The deadly sin of the New Testament is resistance to the Divine operation, while that of the Mazdeans is self-defilement. (S. B. E. IV., p. 101.) The Christian and Buddhist ones are of long retribution, but terminable, for an everlasting hell was not held by the Jews at the time of Christ, and is not implied in the Master's terms. Only the Mazdean uses the language of absolute despair; but if the universalism of the Bundahish be a true tradition from the lost Dâmdâd Nosk, then even this sin is finally forgiven.

Let it not be imagined that the writer has hastily formed the conclusion of a dependence of Christianity upon Buddhism, still less that he regards such dependence as more than occasional. At the very outset of my Indian studies (which began in 1880) I read Rhys Davids' introduction to the Book of the Great Decease (1881) wherein he denounces attempts to trace connection between the two religions. This made a lasting impression on me; and it was not until 1899, when Rendel Harris directed my attention to the Buddhist element in the Acts of Thomas, that the early deterrent of Rhys Davids began to weaken.

Deeper research has since convinced me, not

only of the possibility, but of the probability, of such a connection, albeit in a limited degree. It was during 1899 that I discovered the verbal parallel in John XII. 34. This excited my curiosity and, together with the phrase in Mark, discovered earlier, caused a more systematic search. The search was mostly original, for I made very little use of my predecessors. Indeed the Enunciations and the Logia Book, wherein the chief of my first discoveries were made, had not been translated, and the latter not even now.

In Buddhist and Christian Gospels, p. 49, are these words :—

"I would not, with Seydel, extend the Buddhist influence to the entire Christian Epic, but limit it to the Gospel of Luke, and perhaps John. Even in doing this much, I submit it only as an hypothesis."

In the next edition the last sentence will be cancelled, and the order of Luke and John reversed. The case for John is now stronger than that for Luke.

The Gospels of Luke and John are those which present the most literary finish and betray the widest acquaintance with ancient learning. The German theory of the Lucan authorship is this :— Luke was a follower of Paul, and kept a diary of their travels. This diary was used by the author of the Acts of the Apostles. The Acts is avowedly the second part of the Gospel by the same writer. (Acts I. 1, compared with Luke I. 1-4.) As Luke's diary was largely embedded in the Acts (the "WE Sections") his great name was ascribed to the two books. This was a regular literary practice in those times. Tertullian, a Roman lawyer and one of the most learned of the early Christians, says that the works of disciples are accounted those of their masters. In other words, a book must be heralded by a great name. This principle is not unknown among ourselves. A few years ago a well-known Quaker antiquary wrote a History of Philadelphia, and the publishers ascribed it, on the title-page, to the then librarian of Congress.

It was the aim of the early Church to make each Gospel rest upon apostolic testimony. Mark was called the Gospel of Peter, because Mark was Peter's secretary; and there is no doubt that some scenes in that terse incomparable book are derived from the recollections of the great disciple. Matthew was the penman among the little band, and he, says Papias, compiled the Lord's Oracles or Utterances. True, his original collection has been interwoven, by a later editor, with the biography of Mark, plus certain later legends and minus much of the rugged humanity of the second Evangelist; but Matthew's name is given to the present highly composite production. John died at Ephesus, says a second-century tradition, and the Fourth Gospel emanated from the same metropolis. Doubtless the genius who wrote that divine drama was supplied with certain matter from the son of Zebedee. This would be enough to fasten the latter's name upon the book. Yet the book itself ends with an editorial postscript, as if by several hands:

We know that his testimony is true.

Grotius long ago pointed out that the postscript chapter (John XXI.) must be by a later hand, because it implies the death of the beloved disciple. But the literary principles of antiquity permitted the whole work to pass under the name of the last surviving apostle, whose aged recollections had been the staff of the Evangelist. I am sometimes tempted to regard the Beloved Disciple (so conspicuously absent in the Synoptists) as a Christian imitation of Buddha's Ānando. Indeed it is remarkable that both these beloveds were assured by the Masters of attaining heaven here :—

JOHN APPENDIX (John XXI. 22.)

If I will that he tarry till I come, what is that to thee? (Cf. Mark IX. 1.)

NUMERICAL COLLECTION III. 80.

Even in this life will Ānando enter Nirvana. (12)

Moreover, in the very Buddhist book, The Way to Supernal Knowledge, where the first parallel herein discussed occurs, is a chapter which is quite Johannine. It follows the chapter about the Twin Miracle, and is followed in turn by one about the Lord's omniscience. Mrs. Caroline Rhys Davids has already pointed out the Christian parallelism

(12) Buddhist and Christian Gospels, p. 211.

in this book, I. 54, (13) and I will here translate its most significant features:—

What is the Tathāgato's knowledge of the attainment of the Great Compassion? (14)

Great compassion for creatures descends into the Blessed Buddhas when they see, by many tokens, that the abodes of the world are on fire; that they are on the march, departed, fallen into an evil way. The unstable world is carried along; the world is defenceless, companionless, without goods, when all that is transient is forsaken. Incomplete, unsated is the world, the slave of Thirst; defenceless are the abodes of the world; without shelter, without refuge, without a right path; inflated, unsoothed is the world. The abodes of the world

---

(13) Journal of the Royal Asiatic Society, January, 1906.

(14) The Great Compassion means the Buddha's compassion as distinguished from a disciple's; for every good Buddhist practises the pity-meditation, wherein he projects his mind compassionately toward all creatures. The Great Compassion is a later development of Buddhism, and the Way to Supernal Knowledge is itself a book of the third stage of growth, and really belongs to Abhidhammo. The Island Chronicle says that its canonicity was disputed at the Second Council of the Order, in the fourth century B. C. It is, however, probably later than that. The famous document in the Island Chronicle appears to refer to a quarrel that occurred at the Council of Agnimitra (about 150 B. C.) It is out of place at the Council of Vesāli. (See Sacred Books of the East, Vol. XIX. p. xv.)

have thorns, *are pierced with many thorns, and none can draw them out but I;* flung into a cage of corruption, wrapt in the gloom of ignorance, and there is none can show it light but I. The abodes of the world, given over to ignorance, darkened, enveloped, become as tangled threads, covered with blotches, become as sedge and bulrushes, escape not from doom, perdition, destruction and transmigration....... When the Blessed Buddhas see all these things, the Great Compassion for creatures enters into them, and they say: I have crossed over, but the world has not; I am emancipated, but the world is not; I am subdued, but the world is unsubdued; *I am at peace, but the world is not at peace; comforted, but the world is not comforted;* extinguished, (15) while the world is not. And I who have crossed over, can help others to cross; emancipated, I can set them free; subdued, I can make them self-controlled; *at peace, I can give them peace; comforted, I can console them;* arrived at Nirvana, I can take them thereunto.

The Way to Supernal Knowledge, though not an early book of the Canon, is decidedly pre-Christian. The Abhidharma, wherewith it is a connecting link, was developed between the time of Asoko (and even earlier) and the Christian era. Taka-

(15) Or, *arrived at Nirvana.* Several noble texts in the Sūtras teach us that extinction of egoism is not extinction of the higher personality.

kusu's masterly article in the Journal of the Pâli Text Society for 1905 has made this clear. Some treatise on the Supernal Knowledges was part of the Canon of the Realists, (16) a different sect from that of the Elders who have transmitted to us the Pâli. According to the Realists this treatise existed at the First Council, while the Elders imply the same. We shall know the dates of these books a great deal more precisely when the voluminous Buddhist literature of China is translated. The scholars of Japan are already aroused to the importance of this work, and the names of Nanjio, Takakusu, Minakata, Anesaki and Suzuki will be held in grateful remembrance by students of Buddhism as pioneers in this great undertaking.

The Statement of Knowledges, in the *Way to Supernal Knowledge*, is the section which contains the passages on the miraculous water and the Great Compassion, and it places immediately after them a concluding chapter on the Omniscience of Buddha. This whole section is supported by an ancient table of contents, while succeeding sections are not. It is a curious coincidence that the very sûtra said by the fifth-century commentator to have converted the Greek empire was one on the Buddha's omniscience. (17) Though the Greek

---

(16) See Suzuki's translation, from the Chinese, of the contents of their Canon. (Monist, January, 1904, p. 275.) The Sanskrit term is Pratisa*m*vid.

(17) *The discourse in the Squirrel Park at Sâketa:* Numerical Collection IV. 24. This appears to be the only sermon in the Kâ*l*akârâmo in the Canon.

empire (*Yonaloko*) of the chroniclers meant Bactria, yet literature there current was liable to permeate the Hellenic world. According to the same chroniclers, the Way to Supernal Knowledge was in the Canon committed to writing in Ceylon in the first century B. C. It is not surprising, therefore, that it or a kindred document should be quoted by the Evangelist as writing or Scripture (γραφη).

In the sixties of the first century, when Paul was standing before Nero, Buddhism was being officially welcomed into China. During that memorable decade a Buddhist book (18) was compiled in Chinese and a temple built in its honor. This book was a popular manual long posterior to the sacred texts, which it presupposes. A legendary life of Buddha, akin to the Lalita Vistara, was also translated ; and this too betrays an advanced stage of the Buddhist Holy Writ. The official commentaries of the Indo-Scythian Kanishka, which date from this age or very little later, also presuppose the Pitakas, including the Abhidharma.

The greatest gap in the history of Buddhism is the record of its westward career. Readers of

---

(18) The Sūtra of 42 Sections. Near the beginning we read : "Buddha said : The Arahat is able to fly through the air, change his appearance, *fix the years of his life*, shake heaven and earth." Here we have proof that the doctrine of John XII. 34 was brought into China from India in 67 A. D.

Since the printing of p. 15, my learned friend, Frank Normart, has told me that, in John XII. 34, the Armenian version (fourth century) reads : "The Christ has existed from eternity."

Darwin will remember that in the *Origin of Species* there is a remarkable chapter on the Imperfection of the Geological Record. Indeed it marks an epoch in the science of geology. In like manner the historian of Buddhism (when another century of translations and critiques makes possible his task) will have to write a chapter on the Imperfection of the Record. Two Buddhist countries—Cashmere and Ceylon—were the homes of two ancient sects, the Realists and the Elders; and these have left us recensions of the Canon and extensive commentaries. But from the greater part of India all traces of Buddhism, except ruins, have been swept away. Indeed the Canon and commentaries of Cashmere are preserved only in Chinese and Tibetan translations, with a mere fraction in Sanskrit. Still greater havoc has been wrought in Bactria and Persia, those buffer lands between Buddhadom and Christendom, where both religions contended for the mastery with Mazdeism, until the ruthless hand of Islâm buried all. Some literary relics of these realms are preserved in China and Tibet, and will one day be made known; but it is doubtful whether any connected chronicles, such as those of Ceylon, will be recovered. All records therefore of Greek or Syriac translations have disappeared. There went out a fire from the Korân which consumed them.

Even when translations themselves perish, we sometimes find the fact recorded that they were. This is true of the Greek version of the Avesta, of the Singhalese commentaries on the Pāli texts, and of certain extinct Chinese translations of the life and words of Buddha. But if the Ceylon Chronicles had been lost, we should never have known the existence of the ancient Singhalese commentaries; and if Pliny had been lost, we should not have known that there ever was a Greek Avesta.

Thus we have to thank the Moslem for obliterating the traces of that lost version of the Sūtras which travelled westward. There is no need to postulate a complete version; but it is incredible that Greek Kings like Menander, (19) who inquired into Buddhism, should have been content to let the profound philosophy of Gotamo repose in an unknown tongue when curious Athenians were hungry for news of the celebrated thinkers. What happened when *Barlaam and Joasaph* was carried westward had happened before. Thus, we know from Epiphanius, that Mânî, in the third century, had access to Hindu books of magic. Mânî despatched his disciple Adda to the lands beyond the Euphrates, and in Chinese Turkestan we have now found the fruits of his mission. Moreover, about the year 100, a semi-Mazdean Buddhist book, composed in Parthia, was carried to Rome, and became the scripture of a Christian heresy.

If the apostle Thomas did actually visit Parthia, as Eusebius says, why should he not have brought back with him, on one of his journeys, an Indian book? It is significant that the Gospel of John,

---

(19) Menander's discussion with a Buddhist monk has been translated by Rhys Davids (S. B. E. xxxv, xxxvi.)

wherein our Buddhist passages occur, is the only one of the four that tells anything about Thomas beyond his name in a list. John represents him as a sceptic, and he must therefore have had an intellectual nature which would permit of an interest in Gentile philosophy. But, mere conjecture apart, the fact remains that, since the hymns of Ephrem of Edessa in the fourth century, the name of Thomas has been demonstrably associated, not only with Parthia but with India; and the Gospel and Acts ascribed to him are full of Indian influences. (20)

According to Eusebius, the Gospels were published by the Church in the reign of Trajan (A. D. 98 —117.) Of course, they had existed in some form before this, but this was the date of their authoritative redaction, when the Mark Appendix was added, and (I have given reasons elsewhere for saying) the Matthæan Infancy Section also. (21)

None of these things are stated lightly, but as the result of a lifetime of research. Since 1875, and especially since 1889, I have been a student of the Gospels; for around them my youthful memories are most deeply entwined, and most of my Buddhist studies have been to explain and elucidate them. (22) Had it been in my power to publish my *Documentary Introduction to the Four*

---

(20) See Buddhist and Christian Gospels, Historical Introduction, and Bishop Medlycott's *India and the Apostle Thomas.* (London, 1905.)

(21) Buddhist and Christian Gospels, p. 15.

(22) The Gospels conquered the Sūtras (1) because they

Gospels, written between 1891 and 1898, my present words would have had more weight. (23) The earliest quotations from the Gospels which are there collected, together with the analysis of the books themselves which I made by the aid of Abbott and Rushbrooke, have convinced me that the German theory of their origin is by no means far-fetched. Individual scholars may carry it too far, but on the whole it is true to the facts.

In the main the Gospels are original documents, deriving their inspiration from the life and words of Jesus. But every writer quotes his predecessors and contemporaries, consciously or unconsciously; and these, the most exalted literary works of any age or clime, are no exception.

---

travelled on the larger arc of the missionary circle around the world; (2) because they fell into the hands of the strongest nations; (3) because they were less metaphysical and presented a personal Creator; (4) because the genius of the Hebrews, the Greeks and the Romans made them masterpieces of condensation. The Gospels were written and rewritten within a single century; the Sūtras were elaborated and re-elaborated through half a millennium. But to him who can glean therefrom the pithy oracles of Gotamo, and picture in his mind the sublime life-scenes of the Indian Messiah, the Gospels themselves have a rival. The battle is not over yet, but with the growth of wisdom we shall cease to destroy, and shall preserve the best in both, relegating the Infancy Sections and their like to a juvenile *Basket* of Jātakas and Antilegomena.

(23) The MS. may be consulted at the Historical Society of Pennsylvania. An abstract of it will be found in Buddhist and Christian Gospels, p. iv.

APPENDIX A.

The Buddhist Gospel Scenes on the Great Tope at Anurâdhapura, in the second century, B. C.

Translated from the metrical Great Chronicle of Ceylon (Mahâva*m*so) Chapter 30.

The two lines in red ink are the context of the quotations in John VII. 38 and XII. 34. Those in italics are the subjects of the Miracle Sūtra, uncanonical according to the present Pāli Canon (which owes its final arrangement to Dhātuseno in the fifth century) but evidently considered authentic enough to be pictured in the second century B. C.

Unto the scenes of the Seven Weeks,
Here and there, as he worthy thought,
Due inscriptions the builder made.

1 Brahmâ's prayer he depicted eke,
2 Founding the Spiritual Empire too,
3 Also Yasa's discipleship,
4 Conversion of Bhadra's company,
5 Likewise taming the hermits wild,
6 Bimbisâra's reception eke,
7 Entry into the capital,
8 Taking the Bamboo Forest Park,
9 Also eighty disciples there,
10 Return to Kapilavastu town,

11 Also the jewel cloister there,
12 Nando and Râhulo converts made,
13 Also taking the Victor's Grove,
14 Miracle under the mango-tree,
15 *Preaching in Indra's paradise,*
16 *Miracle of the descent from heaven,*
17 Crowd that the Elder's question made,
18 Text of the Great Concourse divine,
19 Also sermon to Râhulo,
20 Text of Greatest Beatitudes,
21 Crowd around Wealth-guard the elephant,
22, 23 Ā*l*avo, Aŋgulimâlo eke,
24 Taming of Apalâlo too,
25 Pârâyanaka brahmin-throng ;
26 Rejecting the residue of life,
27 Taking the dried-boar offering,
28 Also the gold-cloth pair of robes,
29 Draught of the clarified water eke,
30 Likewise Parinirvâ*n*a too,
31 Lamentation of gods and men,
32 Elder saluting the dead Lord's feet,
33 Kindling and quenching the funeral pyre,
34 Likewise rites that accompanied,
35 Do*n*o dividing the relics eke.

Birth-tales told by the Well-born One
Round about did the architect
Picture to preach to the multitude :

36 Birth Vessantara wrought in full,
38 And all the acts from the Tusitâ City
Unto the Bo-tree's mystic throne.

The last two lines imply the Nativity legends, such as the Angelic Heralds, the prediction of Asito, etc. They are evidently classed with the Jâtakas, which were scattered around everywhere (*yebhuyyena*) to edify the common folk. The bulk of the scenes are from the Major Section on Discipline and the Book of the Great Decease. Bishop Copleston has doubted the genuineness of the Chronicle's account of the sculptures, and thinks it may be fiction. But the following scenes are found at Bharahat and Sâñci, in Central India, two ruins dating from very early times and, roughly speaking, coeval with the Ceylon tope. (24) At Bharahat are Nos. 11 (perhaps), 13, 16, 24, and parts of 37; at Sâñci are Nos. 2, 4, 5, 6, 16, and parts of 37. No. 16, which is both at Bharahat and Sâñci, is the Sa*m*kissa Ladder, i. e. the ladder whereby Buddha descended from heaven at Sa*m*kissa (or Sâ*m*kâçya), after preaching the Gospel to his mother in the other world—another proof of the antiquity of the contents of the Miracle Sūtra. The scene from the Infancy legends common to Bharahat and

---

(24) Grünwedel, in his Buddhist Art in India (English translation, London, 1905, pp. 5 and 23) places both Bharahat and Sāñci gateways in the second century B. C. The gateways are the latest portions of the shrine.

Sâñci is the dream of Buddha's mother about his descent from heaven into her womb. This incident is not in the Pâli Texts on the Marvellous Birth (Long Collection, No. 14; Middling Collection, No. 123) but in the commentaries and other extra-canonical treatises. As I have argued, in Buddhist and Christian Gospels, *if the commentary be older than the Christian era, à fortiori the text is.* Though the Ceylon Chronicles contain many absurdities, yet Indian archæology has confirmed their trustworthiness in main matters. Bishop Copleston admits this, and, applying his principles, I contend for the historicity of the sculptures in question on the ground of their like being found at Bharahat and Sâñci; and these remains are but accidental fractions of the multitude of shrines. They owe their partial preservation to being in out-of-the way places, afar from the destructive Moslem. What care we if the Chronicler says that Asoko built eighty-four thousand topes, when we find half India covered with his ruins? As to Kern's objection about the suspicious duplication of names, how many Christian monks and bishops are named Gregory and Jerome!

In the cases of Nos. 18 and 20, it is probable that the actual texts were graven on the tope. In each case the word *Suttanto* or *Suttam* is used. No. 18 is the twentieth Sûtra in the Pâli Long Collection (Chinese No. 12, according to Takakusu). This text was evidently talismanic, for the Chinese transliterated it, so as to preserve the exact Hindu sounds. Moreover, both this Sûtra, and Nos. 2, 20 and 22 of our list are in the Parittâ, an ancient anthology recited in Ceylon to this day to ward off evil. No. 19 was a favorite text of Asoko's, and it is found in his rock-written list of selections.

In translating the Chronicle's list, I have imitated the rugged metre of the original without any sacrifice of the sense. It is poor poetry from a literary standpoint, the lines being filled out by such easy phrases as *eva ca* ("and also"); but to a student of the Sūtras, to whom every line calls up a vivid picture, this artless catalogue is sublime. (25)

The Great Chronicle relates that delegates from all parts of Buddhadom came to celebrate the Tope's completion, and among them were representatives "from Alexandria, the city of the Greeks." Even if one of the less known Alexandrias be meant, we yet gather from the record that spectators of these sculptured scenes returned to the Greek empire to tell what they had beheld. But Sylvain Lévi of Paris has pointed out that the expression, "Alexandria the city of the Greeks," is regularly used by the Hindu astronomers to mean the Egyptian capital. And from this capital the King of Ceylon had doubtless secured some sculptors, so that nothing would be more natural

(25) Some years ago I copied the Pāli into a pocketbook, and carried it about with me until I knew it by heart. The following note is found beneath it:—"The sublime simplicity of this list of the great Life-Scenes moves me as do the Obsecrations in the Litany. October, 1900"

than for their Alexandrian friends to be represented at the opening. We cannot therefore be surprised if the Evangelists were acquainted with all these scenes and their Scriptural incidents, which would naturally be explained to the pilgrims. Thus, No. 21 is the conspiracy of Devadatto (the Buddhist Judas) against his Master's life, by means of the drunken elephant, upon which occasion the Lord uttered the terrible oracle about the *æon-lasting sin.* (Buddhist and Christian Gospels, Parallel 84). No. 23 is the Penitent Robber (Parallel 28); No. 24 is the taming of a kind of demon; while Nos. 14 and 26 (as we have said above) are the context of the passages in John which are explicitly quoted as Scripture. Neither in the Law, the Prophets nor the Hagiographa of the Jewish Canon do these oracles occur; but both have stood for ages in the Law, or Dharma, of the Buddha.

It is a matter of little moment to our use of the Chronicle's list whether these sculptures were seen by the Chronicler or only imagined. If he imagined them, it was because he knew that these very Gospel scenes were graven upon other monuments of those palmy days; and thousands more besides the Alexandrine delegates to Ceylon had returned to the Roman Empire to tell the story of the Buddha. A profound modern student of Buddhist sculptures has stated his final impression in the following words:—

"Few who are familiar with the arts of Rome in Constantine's time, and who will take the trouble to master these Amarâvatî sculptures, can fail to perceive many points of affinity between them. The circular medallions of the arch of Constantine —such as belong to his time—and the general tone of the art of his age so closely resemble what we find here that the coincidence can hardly be accidental. The conviction that the study of these sculptures has forced on my mind is that *there was much more intercommunication between the East and the West during the period from Alexander to Justinian than is generally supposed; and that the intercourse was especially frequent and influential in the middle period, between Augustus and Constantine.*" [Italics mine].

Thus wrote James Fergusson in 1867, in a note in his *Description of the Amarâvatî Tope*—a note which reappeared in his great work, *Tree and Serpent Worship*. Though many of his conjectures have been invalidated, yet this one, founded upon first-hand study, has been abundantly confirmed. We now know that there is a chain of Greek art reaching all the way from the Adriatic to the Ganges; and the same sculptors who wrought a Buddhist Gospel scene in India could be working later on the arch of Titus. Coins of all the Roman emperors from Augustus to Hadrian are in the museum at Madras, and those of King Gondophares of the Acts of Thomas are also found. The royal agent Abbanes (a good Pâli name, which means Unwounded) who came to Jerusalem seeking an artificer, is not all fiction, for both Christian and Buddhist romances are founded on the facts of ancient life.

APPENDIX B. (NOTES. 7, 8, 9, 10.)

(7) But the Sanskrit Divyvadâna, which preserves a reminiscence of the text, has "flow" :—*adhah kâyam prajvâlayaty, uparimât kâyâc chitalâ vâridhârâh syandante:* "Below his body it blazes ; from his upper body cold torrents flow." These later legends, which took shape in the North of India, after the main body of the Elders had settled in Ceylon (*i. e.* between the third century B. C. and the Christian era) do not present the verbal agreements of the older pericopes. For these verbal agreements, see Burnouf, Lotus de la Bonne Loi, p. 859. The great Buddhist scholar was in the midst of copying passages common to the texts discovered in Nepâl and Ceylon, when his hand was arrested by death (March, 1852). Our science was then put back for half a century.

(8) The Avadânas are semi-canonical. They were only admitted into the Pâli Canon by one school of reciters ; but their presence in later recensions of that Canon and in those of other sects entitles them to be called semi-canonical. The Realists and the Docetists evidently placed them in the Vinaya Pitaka, while the Elders and the Dharmaguptas placed them in a fifth Āgama or Nikâyo, called Short Collection and Miscellaneous Pitaka. The Great Council Canon, which boasted that it was free from "the false additions" of the others, had no Avadânas, but only the germ thereof ; for in its Miscellaneous Pitaka was a book called Nidâna, which is described as "circumstantial notes on Pratyeka-buddhas and Arhats, in gâthâ." (Suzuki). The same book also appears in the Miscellaneous Pitaka of the Dharmaguptas, an early branch of the Elders. This carries the book back behind the final schism at the Council of Agnimitra in the second century B. C.

(9) Sacred Books of the East, Vol. XIX. p. 240. This is the fifth-century Chinese translation, which omits the water-miracle. It is desirable to secure the Tibetan version of this

part of the poem (for the *original* Sanskrit covering this point is lost) and also the Chinese and Tibetan of the Miracle Sūtra in the Realist Vinaya Piṭaka.

(10) The Ceylon tradition makes a mango-tree near Sâvatthi the scene of the miracle. (Spence Hardy, Manual, p. 295.) The water-miracle, however, is omitted in Hardy's account. In view of the fact that the Dīgha reciters rejected the Avadânas, it is quite probable that these were developed among rival sects ; and the *Way to Supernal Knowledge* has borrowed the text about the Twin Miracle from a source outside the Elders' Pâli Canon. In like manner, the Pâli commentaries, at a later date, were amplified by Buddhaghoso, who came from continental India. Many of the Avadâna legends which had grown up there after the main body of the Elders had developed a local individuality in the Dekhan and Ceylon are included in these commentaries ; and the *Way to Supernal Knowledge* is a late treatise, standing midway between the Sūtras and the commentaries. Its canonicity was denied by the Great Council school, probably at the Council of Agnimitra, about 150 B. C. (The Island Chronicle document is evidently misplaced, for there were no "six books of the Abhidhammo" at the Council of Vesâli.)

CONCLUSION.

Already in the eighteenth century Michaelis discerned a Zoroastrian and a Sabian influence in John; so that our present thesis is no radically new departure.

Had the Evangelist used without ascription the phrases and doctrines herein set forth, we might consider them due to a community of Oriental ideas; but his express quotations of two of them as Law and Scripture compel the inference that they existed in some sacred literature of the Apostolic age. The only known source of the two quoted texts is the Buddhist Canon, which in the first Christian century was the most widespread of all sacred codes—covering even a vaster field than its great rivals, the Septuagint and the Zend Avesta (26) and being the dominant religious force upon the continent of Asia.

---

(26) The extent of Mazdeism (including the Mithra cult) at the end of the first century is roughly indicated by the cities of York, Cabul and Cadiz; that of Buddhism, by Cabul, Honan and Anurâdhapura; that of Judaism and rising Christianity by Marseilles, Cadiz, and Ecbatana. But the diffusion and active copying of the sacred canons puts Mazdeism out of the race, for the Avesta was already crippled and little known. (The Greek version of Hermippus was probably confined to Alexandria). Of those purely national codes, the Vedas and the Confucian Classics, we are not speaking, though Buddhism carried a partial knowledge of the former, and the Chinese arms had probably spread a knowledge of the latter. As to Buddhism and Christianity, while the impetus of the one was eastward and the other westward from the lands of their birth, yet there was a retrograde movement in each case, comparable to the rebound of a gun. These rebounds were felt in the Parthian empire, the home of Mazdeism, which was therefore the theatre of the most complex religious forces.

BUDDHIST AND CHRISTIAN GOSPELS

now first compared from the originals:
being "Gospel Parallels from Pâli Texts,"
reprinted with additions.

By Albert J. Edmunds,

Honorary Member of the International Buddhist Society of Rangūn, translator of the Dhammapada, the Buddhist Genesis, &c., member of the Oriental Club of Philadelphia.

Third and Complete Edition.

Edited, with Parallels and Notes
from the Chinese Buddhist Tripiṭaka,

by M. Anesaki,

Professor of Religious Science in the Imperial University of Tōkyō.

Tōkyō:
The Yūhōkwan Publishing House
1905.

Note.—This book appeared on May 27, 1905. Opinions of scholars will be found in the Appendix to *Fairmount Park and other Poems* (Philadelphia, 1906.) The whole edition is really proof-copy, which the author never corrected, on account of distance. Even the title is misprinted, but the above is its correct form. Corrected copies were presented to the National Library at Washington, in hopes that the card catalogue slips, which are distributed throughout the States, would show the true title. But the rules of bibliography require that the blunder of an Asiatic printer should be perpetuated rather than the writing of the author. This comes of our superstitious regard for print.

ERRATA et Corrigenda.

Frontispiece.	For *Pàli* read *Pâli.*
P. 10, line 15.	For *preceeding* read *proceeding.*
P. 17, line 11.	For *Mahavaggo* read *Mahâvaggo.*
" " " "	For *Nalaka* read *Nâlaka.*
P. 31, line 8.	For *Those in italics,* read *Nos. 14, 15 and 16.*
P. 38, line 2.	For *Divyvadâna* read *Divyâvadâna.*

Owing to the contingencies of Philadelphia type-foundries, the bar and the circumflex have been used indiscriminately to mark long vowels.